T·H·E
ORANGES

5c

T·H·E B·E·S·T O·F
ORANGES

GARAMOND

First published by Garamond Ltd, Publishers
Strode House, 44–50 Osnaburgh Street, London NW1 3ND

Copyright © Garamond Ltd, Publishers 1990

ISBN 1–85583–030–2

Illustrations by Madeleine David

Printed and bound in UK by MacLehose and Partners Ltd.
Typeset by Bookworm Ltd.

CONTENTS

INTRODUCTION

The evergreen orange tree, with its dark, glossy leaves and scented blossom, is probably the best known of all the citrus family. China is thought to be the home of the sweet orange and India the home of the bitter variety. The species has a number of synonyms, but all oranges share the name *hespiridium*, from the Roman goddess Hesperides, who was thought to have brought the orange across the seas to Italy.

Goddess or sailor-borne, the first arrival was the bitter orange, an ornamental shrub with sour, inedible fruit. The flowers and leaves are very aromatic, with a heady, lasting scent which can carry for miles. A mature tree can yield up to 27 kilograms (60 lbs) of blossom in a season. The white flowers are traditionally used in wedding bouquets and pot pourri mixtures, and orange-flower water – much beloved of French and English pastrycooks as a flavouring for cakes and dessert pastries – is used in cosmetics as well. The rind of the bitter orange is also valuable, providing *neroli*, or orange oil, and is used in many orange-flavoured liqueurs, such as Curaçao and Grand Marnier.

The sour Seville orange was traditionally brought to Spain by the Moors, who forbade any unbeliever to taste one until he was converted to Islam. The juice was thought to be an aid to digestion, and today the Spanish groves are a picturesque but highly commercialized industry. Seville oranges, small and sharply flavoured, are favourites for the traditional English marmalade. They can be combined with their cousins in the citrus family – grapefruit or tangerines – to produce delicious variations on the marmalade theme. The bergamot orange is a separate cultivar; its special contribution is the oil that is processed from the rind and used in cosmetics and perfumes.

The sweet orange found its way across Europe first with the Romans and then with the Portuguese East Indian traders in the fifteenth and sixteenth centuries. Spanish ships on their way to colonies in the New World were required to carry orange seeds and young trees for the new plantations. Today, there are huge orange groves in North Africa, Israel, Florida and California. In the tropics, the fruit stays green.

Although there are many individual varieties, sweet oranges fall mainly into three categories: blondes or normal oranges, the most common; smaller blood oranges, their darker flesh flecked with reddish spots which may indeed tint the entire fruit; and navel oranges, with a prominent growth at the stem end – often an entire, miniature, undeveloped orange in itself. The navel has become the most popular orange for eating raw as it peels easily and can be divided into segments with the fingers. The rind or zest contains enough oil to intensify any orange flavour in a dish. Rub the rind with a cube of sugar to absorb the oil, and add the crushed cube to the other ingredients. The peel can be candied for use in cakes, and any of the sweet or bitter oranges can be stuck with cloves and powdered with orris root to make sweet-smelling pomanders.

Orange segments (with all the pith removed) can be sugar frozen; use 225 grams (8 oz) caster sugar for every 450 grams (1 lb) of fruit. Freeze Seville oranges whole in plastic bags. Grated peel can also be frozen.

As everyone knows, oranges are full of Vitamin C – one sweet orange supplies the average adult with enough of this important vitamin for one day. They also have valuable cosmetic properties. Orange-flower water soothes the skin, and orange oil is an important constituent in many creams and perfumes.

DUCKLING WITH ORANGE

---

1 oven-ready duckling about 2.3 kilograms (5 lbs)
50 grams (2 oz) butter
Salt and freshly ground black pepper
3 Seville oranges
2 lemons
150 millilitres (¼ pint) dry white vermouth
2 large sweet oranges
1 tablespoon sugar
1 tablespoon wine vinegar
½ tablespoon cornflour
2 tablespoons orange liqueur
(optional, see method)
2 tablespoons redcurrant jelly
1 tablespoon orange marmalade, preferably Seville
Thin slices of sweet orange and watercress sprigs, to garnish

---

In a flameproof roasting tin, brown duckling all over in foaming butter, taking care butter does not burn. When bird is uniformly crisp and brown all over, sprinkle it with salt and freshly ground black pepper.

Roast duckling in a moderate oven (180°C, 350°F, Mark 4) for 45–60 minutes or until juices run clear when a skewer is pushed into the thickest part of the leg, closest to the breast. Baste regularly with pan juices and take care not to overcook duck as this will make it dry and tasteless.

While duck is roasting, peel Seville oranges with a potato peeler, taking only the coloured rind (*no* pith). Cut rind into fine, hair-thin strips. Put them in a pan with plenty of water to cover, bring slowly to boiling point, drain thoroughly and put aside until needed. Then cut oranges in half, squeeze out all their juice and strain into a large, wide-necked jug. Squeeze juice from lemons and strain into jug. Stir in dry vermouth.

Peel sweet oranges and, working over jug to catch juices, cut out segments. Remove pips with the point of your knife. Squeeze all remaining juices from orange piths into jug.

When duckling is done, transfer it to a heated serving dish. Return it to the switched-off oven with the door left slightly ajar to keep hot while you finish garnish and sauce.

In a small, heavy pan, swirl sugar and vinegar together over moderate heat until sugar melts and turns into a rich golden caramel. Immediately pour in contents of jug, stirring until caramel has dissolved. Then add prepared orange segments and poach gently for 5 minutes. With a slotted spoon, lift orange segments out and arrange them carefully around duckling.

Pour off all but 1 or 2 tablespoons of fat from roasting tin. Pour in citrus syrup and slowly bring to boiling point, stirring and scraping bottom and sides of pan clean with a wooden spoon.

Blend cornflour smoothly with orange liqueur (or use water if you have no liqueur available). Stir into roasting tin and simmer for 2 or 3 minutes, stirring, until sauce is slightly thickened and no longer cloudy. Stir in blanched orange zest, redcurrant jelly and orange marmalade, simmering until melted. Season generously with salt and freshly ground black pepper.

Spoon some of the sauce over duckling and pour remainder into a heated sauceboat. Decorate dish with paper-thin slices of fresh sweet orange and sprigs of watercress. Serve with sauce.

Serves 4

MOROCCAN SPICED LAMB

2.51.4–1.6 kilograms (3–3½ lbs) lean lamb, cubed
1 teaspoon ground cinnamon
½ teaspoon ground cloves
Salt
4 tablespoons peanut or corn oil
2 Spanish onions, finely chopped
1 clove garlic, finely chopped
A 5 centimetre (2 in.) piece of fresh ginger root, peeled and finely chopped
2–3 sprigs parsley
1 sprig thyme
150 millilitres (¼ pint) dry white wine
Finely grated rind and juice of 2–3 oranges
Freshly ground black pepper
1 teaspoon flour
1 teaspoon French mustard

Sprinkle cubes of lamb with a mixture of cinnamon, cloves and 2 teaspoons salt, turning them round to coat them on all sides. In a heavy, flameproof casserole over moderate heat, fry spiced lamb cubes, a portion at a time, in about half the oil until golden brown on all sides, transferring them to a plate with a slotted spoon as they are done.

In the remaining oil, sauté finely chopped onions with garlic and ginger until soft and golden. Return lamb to casserole. Add parsley and thyme sprigs tied together in a bouquet, and mix well. Moisten with wine and orange juice, and stir in grated orange rind. Finally, stir in about

300 millilitres (½ pint) water and season generously with freshly ground black pepper. Slowly bring to simmering point. Stir once more, cover and cook very gently until lamb is tender, about 45–60 minutes.

Blend flour and mustard smoothly with 2 or 3 tablespoons water. Stir into casserole. Mix well with sauce and bring to simmering point once more. Cook gently, stirring frequently, until sauce has thickened.

Discard herb bouquet. Correct seasoning with more salt or freshly ground black pepper if necessary and serve.

Serves 6 – 8

THAI ORANGE AND PORK SALAD

4 large, sweet oranges
1 crisp head lettuce
125–175 grams (4–6 oz) lean raw pork, trimmed
1 plump clove garlic, crushed
2 tablespoons peanut or other cooking oil
1 tablespoon finely chopped peanuts
1 teaspoon sugar
2 tablespoons dark soya sauce
Pinch of monosodium glutamate
Pinch of paprika
Salt and freshly ground black pepper
Finely chopped parsley, chives or spring onion tops, to garnish

Peel and segment oranges, working over a plate to catch any juices and discarding pips as you come across them. Take lettuce apart. Wash and pat leaves dry individually. Lay them, torn up if they are large, on a serving platter. Arrange orange sections on top and sprinkle with any juices you have saved. Put aside while you prepare dressing.

Cut pork into small, thin strips, discarding any fat or gristle
as you come across it.

In a large frying pan, sauté garlic in oil until golden but
not burned (this could make it bitter). Add pork strips and
stir-fry until lightly coloured all over. Stir in chopped
peanuts and continue to stir-fry for a minute or two
longer. Sprinkle with sugar, soya sauce and 2 tablespoons
water. Mix well. Season with monosodium glutamate and
paprika, and a little ordinary salt and/or freshly ground
black pepper to taste if liked. Continue to stir-fry for a few
minutes longer until pork is thoroughly cooked and sauce
reduced.

Pour hot contents of pan over oranges and lettuce.
Sprinkle with chopped parsley, chives or spring onion tops.
Serve cold.

Serves 4

FRESH ORANGE AND DATE SALAD

100–125 grams (4 oz) dried dates
3 tablespoons salad oil
1 tablespoon lemon juice
Salt
2 juicy oranges
Lettuce leaves and finely chopped walnuts, to garnish

Cover dates with boiling water and leave to soften and plump up for about 10 minutes. Then drain dates thoroughly, stone them and cut into small pieces. In a bowl, beat oil and lemon juice together with a pinch of salt.
Add dates and toss with a fork until well mixed.

Peel oranges, removing every scrap of white pith. Cut them horizontally into thin slices, picking out and discarding pips as you come across them.

Line a serving platter or bowl with lettuce leaves. Arrange orange slices on them and spoon dates and dressing over the top. Sprinkle with a few chopped walnuts and serve.

Serves 4–6

ORANGE RICE WITH ALMONDS

---

1 teaspoon whole coriander seeds
1 medium-sized onion, finely chopped
3–4 stalks celery, diagonally sliced
100–125 grams (4 oz) butter
1 tablespoon finely grated orange rind
2 cups (about 350 grams or ¾ lb) long-grain rice
2 cups (about 400 millilitres or ¾ pint) each well-flavoured chicken stock and fresh orange juice
Salt
Sautéed slivered almonds, to garnish

In a mortar, crush coriander seeds finely with a pestle. Put aside.

Choose a large, heatproof casserole with a tight-fitting lid. In it, fry the onion and celery gently in half the butter until quite soft but only lightly coloured. Add the crushed coriander seeds, orange rind and the remaining butter, and when this has melted, stir in the rice. Cook gently, stirring, until each grain is coated with butter. Then add chicken stock, orange juice and salt, to taste. Bring to boiling point, stirring, then lower heat to a bare simmer, cover tightly and cook for 20 minutes, or until rice grains are tender and all the liquid has been absorbed. '

Heap rice into a heated dish.

Sprinkle sautéed almonds over the top and serve.

Serves 6–8

GLAZED CABBAGE À L'ORANGE

1 large, juicy orange
1 small white cabbage
1 Spanish onion, finely chopped
50 grams (2 oz) butter
6–8 tablespoons chicken (cube) stock
Salt and freshly ground black pepper
2–3 tablespoons currants (optional)
1–2 tablespoons soft brown sugar

Grate orange rind finely. Then peel orange and cut out segments. Discard any pips and cut each segment in 2 or 3. Work over a dish to catch all the juice which may drip out and add orange segments to dish. Quarter, core and shred cabbage finely. Put it in a colander and slowly pour a kettle of boiling water over it. Shake off as much water as possible and put aside until needed.

In a heavy, flameproof casserole or saucepan, sauté onion gently in butter until soft and golden. Stir in shredded cabbage and continue to sauté for a minute or two longer until shreds are coated with butter. Mix in grated orange rind. Moisten with chicken stock and any juice that has drained from orange segments. Season to taste with salt, grind in some pepper, cover and cook gently until cabbage has softened, about 20 minutes. Then mix in pieces of orange and currants, if used, and sprinkle with sugar. Correct seasoning with a little more salt or freshly ground black pepper. Continue to cook gently, stirring frequently, until sugar has melted and is beginning to look slightly caramelized.

Keep hot, covered, until ready to serve.

Serves 4–6

GINGERED RICE

40 grams (1½ oz) butter
1 medium onion, finely chopped
1 cup long-grain rice
Finely grated rind of 1 orange
½ teaspoon ground ginger
½ cup fresh orange juice
1½ cups well-flavoured chicken (cube) stock
Finely chopped parsley, to garnish

In a heavy pan, melt butter and fry onion gently until soft and golden. Stir in rice and continue to fry, stirring, until each grain is shiny with butter and lightly coloured. Stir in orange rind and ginger, mix well and fry for a minute or two longer. Remove pan from heat and cool slightly.

Stir in orange juice and chicken stock. Bring to boiling point, stir once and lower heat to a bare simmer. Cover pan tightly and cook gently for 15–20 minutes (without lifting the lid once) until all the liquid is absorbed and rice grains are fluffy and separate. Garnish with parsley.

Serves 4

SUNSHINE SOUFFLÉ

1 tablespoon unflavoured powdered gelatine
4 eggs, separated
175 grams (6 oz) caster sugar
Finely grated rinds of 1 orange and 1 lemon
Juice of 3–4 oranges
Juice of 1 lemon

Sprinkle gelatine over 3 or 4 tablespoons cold water in a small cup. Then, when the gelatine has absorbed the water and set, stand the cup in a pan of hot water, stirring until the liquid is clear. Allow to cool to room temperature.

In a large bowl, whisk the egg yolks, sugar and grated rinds together until thick and fluffy. Stir the gelatine into the orange and lemon juices, then gradually whisk into the egg yolk mixture. Leave until syrupy.

Whisk the egg whites until stiff but not dry. Fold them gently into the mixture. Spoon it into a serving bowl and chill until set.

Serves 6

CRÊPES SUZETTE

12–16 small, thin pancakes
100–125 grams (4 oz) unsalted butter
6 tablespoons caster sugar
Finely grated rind of 1 large orange
6 tablespoons fresh orange juice
1 teaspoon lemon juice
5 tablespoons Curaçao or Cointreau
2 tablespoons brandy

Prepare pancakes in advance and stack them on an upturned soup plate under a cloth to keep them soft and pliable. The orange butter may also be made in advance and stored in the refrigerator until needed.

Cream butter and gradually add 5 tablespoons caster sugar, beating vigorously until mixture is white and fluffy. Beat in grated orange rind, then slowly beat in orange and lemon juice, followed by 2 tablespoons of the orange liqueur. Do not worry if butter looks curdled at this stage. Scrape it all out into a bowl and chill until you are ready to use it.

Fry pancakes in orange butter either in a large, heavy frying pan, preferably one with rounded sides so pancakes will slip out easily, or in a chafing dish at the table. First place the remaining orange liqueur and the brandy in a small pan, ready to heat up and set alight when needed. Next, melt orange butter in frying pan. Place the first pancake flat in the bubbling hot butter, submerging it totally, then fold it in four and push it to one side. Repeat with remaining pancakes. Then distribute them all evenly over surface of pan and allow to bubble gently while you proceed to the final stage.

Sprinkle pancakes with remaining tablespoon of caster sugar. Gently heat pan of brandy and liqueur, and when fumes start rising, carefully put a match to it. As soon as flames are well established, pour all over pancakes. Take pan from the heat and keep shaking it gently and spooning buttery syrup over pancakes until flames die out. Serve immediately.

Serves 4–6

PETITS POTS DE CHOCOLAT GRAND MARNIER

100–125 grams (4 oz) good-quality dark, bitter chocolate
25 grams (1 oz) unsalted butter
2 thin-skinned oranges
Grand Marnier, Curaçao or brandy
2 eggs, separated

Break the chocolate up into the top of a double saucepan, and add the butter. Cut 1 orange into chunks, saving juice; remove pips and blend orange finely; add its juice and blend the two together thoroughly. Add to the chocolate. Stir over hot water until chocolate has melted and mixture is smooth. Remove top of pan, cool slightly and stir in 1 tablespoon orange liqueur or brandy.

In a bowl, whisk egg yolks until fluffy. Strain in the chocolate mixture, whisking constantly. Whisk egg whites until stiff but not dry and fold into the chocolate mixture. Pour into individual little pots, custard cups or soufflé dishes; allow to become quite cold and chill until ready to serve.

Just before serving, cut 2 large, thin slices from the centre of the second orange. Quarter them by making two crosswise cuts through each slice and lay two quarters point to point on top of each portion to make a bow-tie shape. Finally, pour a little more liqueur over the surface of each pot, just enough to make it look glossy.

Serves 4

CHEESEBREAD

350 grams (12 oz) plain wholewheat flour
50 grams (2 oz) soft dark brown sugar
1 teaspoon ground cinnamon
½ teaspoon salt
¼ teaspoon bicarbonate of soda
225 grams (8 oz) cottage cheese
Finely grated rind of 1 orange
1 teaspoon vanilla essence
1 egg
25 grams (1 oz) fresh yeast or 15 grams (½ oz) dried yeast
6 tablespoons orange juice
75 grams (3 oz) raisins
Margarine, for loaf tin

Stir the flour, sugar, cinnamon, salt and soda together until well mixed. Rub the cottage cheese through a sieve into another bowl and beat in the orange rind and vanilla essence. Beat the egg until foamy. Dissolve fresh yeast in orange juice (if using dried yeast, follow packet directions).

Make a well in the centre of the flour mixture. Add all the remaining ingredients except the raisins and margarine, and knead vigorously until the dough tends to leave the sides of the bowl clean (it will be very sticky). Work in the raisins so they are well distributed throughout the dough. Cover the bowl with a cloth and leave the dough to rise until doubled in bulk.

Grease a 900 gram (2 lb) loaf tin with margarine. Deflate the dough, knead lightly and transfer it to the loaf tin, which it will half-fill. Cover the tin with a cloth and leave the dough until doubled in bulk again. Then bake bread in a moderate oven (190°C, 375°F, Mark 5) for 35 minutes, or until it is well risen and a thin skewer pushed through the centre feels dry to the touch.

Let the loaf cool in its baking tin, lying on its side on a cooling rack. Then remove the tin and let the loaf cool completely, still on its side, before storing (till the following day if possible).

WALNUT CAKE

100–125 grams (4 oz) walnuts
3 tablespoons plain flour
1 teaspoon baking powder
Generous pinch of salt
1 medium orange
4 eggs, separated
150 grams (5 oz) caster sugar
3 tablespoons melted butter
Walnut halves, to decorate

Chocolate icing
100–125 grams (4 oz) bitter dessert chocolate
2 tablespoons melted butter

Grind the walnuts finely in a blender or food processor. (Do not use a meat mincer, which tends to make the nuts too oily.) Mix the ground nuts thoroughly with the flour, baking powder and salt. Grate the rind of the orange finely and mix into the flour mixture.

Beat egg yolks until thick and lemon-coloured, then gradually beat in 90 grams (3½ oz) caster sugar. Fold in the walnut mixture, followed by the juice of ½ the orange.

In another bowl, whisk the egg whites until they form soft, floppy peaks. Gradually add the remaining sugar, whisking constantly to make a stiff meringue. With a large metal spoon, fold meringue into yolk mixture.

Spoon cake mixture gently into a well-buttered, deep 20 centimetre (8 in) cake tin. Bake in a moderate oven

(180°C, 350°F, Mark 4) for 40 minutes, or until the cake is a rich golden colour, feels firm when pressed lightly and has shrunk away slightly from the sides of the tin. Allow the cake to cool in its tin on a rack for 10 minutes before turning it out on to the rack and leaving it until cold.

To make chocolate icing, break the chocolate into small pieces. Put it in a heatproof bowl, stand the bowl in simmering water and leave until chocolate has melted, stirring frequently. Beat in the butter and continue to beat until smooth.

Spread icing over top and sides of cake with a broad-bladed knife. Decorate with walnut halves. Leave until icing has become dry to the touch.

ABERDEEN
SHORTBREAD

---

50 grams (2oz) soft brown sugar
90 grams (3½ oz) soft margarine
Finely grated rind of 1 large orange
150 grams (5 oz) unbleached plain flour
25 grams (1 oz) cornflour
1 teaspoon baking powder

If you have a food processor, put all the ingredients in it together, switch on, and your ball of dough will be ready in a couple of minutes.

Otherwise, cream the sugar with the margarine and the finely grated orange rind. Sift the flour, cornflour and baking powder together, and combine with the sugar mixture to make a firm dough. Roll into a ball, wrap in plastic and chill for 1 hour.

Dust a board and your rolling pin *very* lightly with flour and roll the dough out about 3 millimetres (⅛ in.) thick. Stamp out biscuits with a 5 centimetre (2 ins.) pastry cutter and carefully, with a spatula, transfer them to lightly greased baking sheets. Prick each biscuit two or three times with the tines of a fork.

Bake the biscuits in a moderate oven (180°C, 350°F, Mark 4) for 25 minutes, or until a rich golden colour. Allow them to cool a little on the baking sheets before transferring to wire racks. When quite cold, store in an airtight tin or jar.

ELIZABETHAN SWEETMEATS

2 large thin-skinned oranges
225 grams (8 oz) sugar
1 centre slice lemon
2 tablespoons Grand Marnier, Curaçao or brandy (optional)

Wash the oranges and dry them thoroughly. Carefully strip off the peel from each orange in eight sections. If the white pith is thick, shave it down with a sharp knife. Roll the peels up tightly and thread them side by side to make a 'necklace', using a large needle and a length of strong thread. Tie the ends of thread together.

In an enamelled pan, cover the necklace of rinds with cold water and bring to a rapid boil. Drain and repeat twice more. The third time, continue to boil gently until the peels are quite soft, 10–15 minutes. Drain thoroughly and pat dry with paper towels.

Rinse the pan and in it dissolve the sugar in 300 millilitres (½ pint) water, together with the lemon slice. Stir in the liqueur or brandy, if used. Skim off scum if necessary. Add the rinds and simmer gently until they are very soft and the syrup is thick, 20–30 minutes. Cool in the pan, covered. Remove the lemon slice, unthread the orange rolls and pack them into a glass jar. Pour over the syrup, cover the jar and store in a cool, dark cupboard.

MALTAISE

3 egg yolks
1–2 tablespoons lemon juice
Salt and white pepper
175 grams (6 oz) unsalted butter
Finely grated rind of ½ orange
Juice of 1 small orange

In the top of a double saucepan, or a bowl that fits snugly
over (*not* in) a pan of simmering water, beat egg yolks with
a tablespoon each of lemon juice and water, a good pinch
of salt and a generous dash of white pepper.
Divide butter into 10 or 12 cubes and leave on a plate to
soften slightly without turning oily.
Fit top of double saucepan or bowl over simmering water.
Drop in the first piece of butter and beat lightly by hand

with a wire whisk until it is incorporated into egg yolks. Beat in one or two more pieces of butter in the same way, taking great care that sauce does not overheat, or it will curdle. If it looks in any danger of separating, immediately lift the top container off and quickly beat in a tablespoon of cold water to lower the temperature of the sauce slightly, beating vigorously until it is quite smooth again.

With the pan off the heat, continue to beat in butter, a piece at a time. Then flavour sauce with grated orange rind and thin it down slightly with orange juice. Finally, taste and adjust flavour of sauce with more salt, white pepper or orange juice as desired.

Keep sauce hot until ready to serve by standing it over hot (*not* boiling) water. Give it an occasional stir, paying particular attention to the bottom and corners of the pan.

Serve sauce in a heated sauceboat.

Serves 4–6

TRADITIONAL ENGLISH MARMALADE

900 grams (2 lbs) Seville oranges
2 lemons
1.8 kilograms (4 lbs) sugar
Small knob of butter or margarine
(optional)

Scrub the oranges and lemons thoroughly under the cold tap. Pack them in a pressure cooker with 550 millilitres (1 pint) water, bring to 7 kilograms (15 lbs) pressure and cook for 15 minutes if oranges are very large, only 10 minutes if smaller. Reduce pressure.

Open the cooker and lift out the fruit with a slotted spoon. When they are cool enough to handle, cut them in half and with a sharp-edged teaspoon scrape all the pulp, pith and seeds out of the peels into a bowl. Stir this back into the water remaining in the cooker and boil hard for 10 minutes.

Meanwhile, slice the peels in half again lengthwise and cut them into matchstick strips.

Strain the boiled liquid through a fine sieve. For a crystal-clear jelly, line the sieve with double-thick muslin and allow as much liquid as possible to drip through without squeezing or pressing through any pulp. However, if this is not important, press the pulp lightly against the sides of the sieve with the back of a wooden spoon to extract as much liquid as possible. Pour it back into the cooker.

Add sugar and stir with a wooden spoon over low heat until dissolved. Stir in shredded peel and boil briskly until setting point is reached. A small knob of butter or margarine stirred in at the last moment will take care of any scum.

Cool for 5 minutes and pour hot into hot, dry jars. Cover immediately and leave until quite cold before storing.

Fills about 7 jars

NORFOLK WINE

1 large orange
1 tablespoon whole cloves
½ teaspoon ground cinnamon
½ teaspoon ground cloves
½ teaspoon allspice
1 blade mace
15 grams (½ oz) root ginger, peeled and finely chopped
1.1 litres (2 pints) non-vintage port
75 grams (3 oz) granulated sugar
Juice of 1 lemon
Nutmeg

Pre-heat the oven to cool (120°C, 250°F, Mark ¼). Stud the orange all over with the whole cloves. Place on a baking tray and cook in the oven for about 1 hour.

Then, put all the spices and 300 millilitres (½ pint) water in a medium saucepan. Bring to the boil and simmer until the water is reduced by half. In a separate large saucepan, heat the port until almost boiling.

Remove from the heat. Strain the spiced water through a fine sieve on to the port. Add the baked orange. Return the pan to the heat and cook slowly for 10 minutes, but do not allow to boil.

When ready to serve, put the sugar and lemon juice in a punch bowl. Pour over the hot, spiced port. Stir and grate some nutmeg over the surface. Serve hot, by ladling into warm glasses.

Serves 6

FRESH ORANGEADE

225 grams (8 oz) sugar
Grated rind and juice of 2 large oranges
Juice of 1 lemon
Soda water
Orange slices, to decorate

Place the sugar and 900 millilitres (1½ pints) water in a pan. Heat gently, stirring, until the sugar dissolves, but do not boil. Pour into a 1.1 litre (2 pint) jug. Add the rind and juices to the jug, stir, cover and leave to stand in a cool place for 3 hours. Strain off the rind and chill in the refrigerator until wanted. To serve, two-thirds fill a tall chilled glass then top up with soda water and ice. Decorate each serving with a thin slice of orange.

ORANGE-FLOWER
BATH OIL

It is easy to make your own orange-flower bath oil, given a reasonable supply of sunlight.

Put the flowers (the leaves can be added too) into a glass jar and pour enough oil to cover them. Any unscented oil is suitable; olive oil is often recommended and almond oil, though expensive, is superb. A little wine or cider vinegar – a tablespoon to 300 millilitres (½ pt) – will help preserve it. Seal the jar and stand it in a sunny place for 2–3 weeks, shaking it twice a day. Strain the oil and repeat with fresh flowers. The process may need repeating 2 or 3 times before the oil is strongly enough scented.

SKIN LOTION

Orange-flower water is a soothing skin lotion, and not as astringent as lemon. Make a distillation, or add a few drops of essential oil of orange flowers (also called oil of neroli) to some distilled water. This will improve after a week or two, but will not keep indefinitely. Mix with glycerine – about 1 part glycerine to 3 or 4 of orange-flower water – to make a gentle toning lotion.

POMANDER

Exotic-smelling pomanders perfume clothes and keep away moths.

Mark an orange into quarters, and use a knitting needle to make holes all over the skin, leaving enough space at the quarter marks to tie a ribbon around the orange. Press cloves firmly into the holes.

Now put the pomander in a paper bag with powdered orris root, which will 'fix' the spicy fragrance, and shake it until well covered. Then store it in a warm, dry, dark place, still in its bag, for a fortnight or so to dry out. Tie a pretty ribbon round it and make a loop for hanging it up.

REMEDIES

Long before the importance of Vitamin C was understood, oranges, especially the bitter variety, were used for various medicinal purposes.

True orange-flower water, made from essence of orange flowers, is an excellent sedative. An infusion of dried orange flowers, though not so potent, is still effective, as are infusions and decoctions of the leaves.

The distilled oil of orange blossom is said to have a hypnotic effect when inhaled.

MEASUREMENTS

Quantities have been given in both metric and imperial measures in this book. However, many foodstuffs are now available only in metric quantities; the list below gives metric measures for weight and liquid capacity, and their imperial equivalents used in this book.

WEIGHT

25 grams	1 oz
50 grams	2 oz
75 grams	3 oz
100–125 grams	4 oz
150 grams	5 oz
175 grams	6 oz
200 grams	7 oz
225 grams	8 oz
250 grams	9 oz
275 grams	10 oz
300 grams	11 oz
350 grams	12 oz
375 grams	13 oz

400 grams	14 oz
425 grams	15 oz
450 grams	1 lb
500 grams (½ kilogram)	1 lb 1½ oz
1 kilogram	2 lb 3 oz
1.5 kilograms	3 lb 5 oz
2 kilograms	4 lb 6 oz
2.5 kilograms	5 lb 8 oz
3 kilograms	6 lb 10 oz
3.5 kilograms	7 lb 11 oz
4 kilograms	8 lb 13 oz
4.5 kilograms	9 lb 14 oz
5 kilograms	11 lb

LIQUID CAPACITY

150 millilitres	¼ pint
300 millilitres	½ pint
425 millilitres	¾ pint
550–600 millilitres	1 pint
900 millilitres	1½ pints
1000 millilitres (1 litre)	1¾ pints
1.2 litres	2 pints
1.3 litres	2¼ pints
1.4 litres	2½ pints
1.5 litres	2¾ pints
1.9 litres	3¼ pints
2 litres	3½ pints
2.5 litres	4½ pints

OVEN TEMPERATURES

Very low	130°C, 250°F, Mark ½
Low	140°C, 275°F, Mark 1
Very slow	150°C, 300°F, Mark 2
Slow	170°C, 325°F, Mark 3
Moderate	180°C, 350°F, Mark 4
	190°C, 375°F, Mark 5
Moderately hot	200°C, 400°F, Mark 6
Fairly hot	220°C, 425°F, Mark 7
Hot	230°C, 450°F, Mark 8